Kosher C...

A Jewish Mandala Coloring Book

Symbols of Jewish holidays with intricate patterns and funny sayings

PeakSeason COLORING

This Book Belongs To:

_____

© 2019, Peak Season Coloring. ALL RIGHTS RESERVED. This one copy is for personal use only and no part of this product may be reproduced or used for commercial purposes.

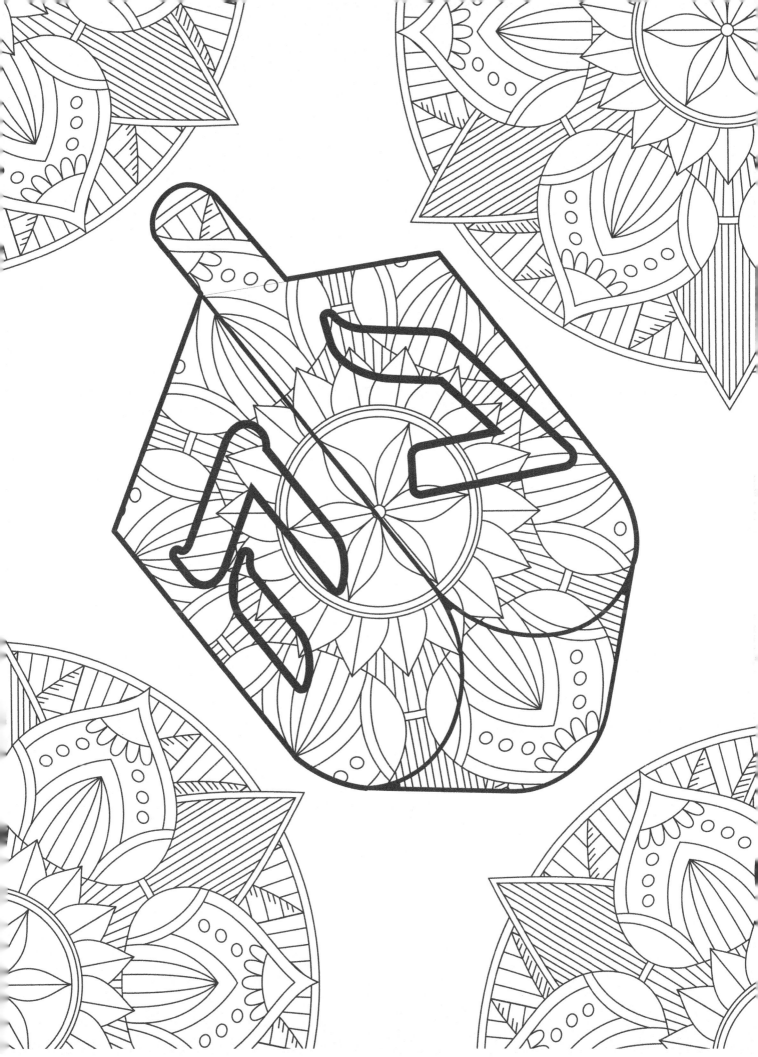

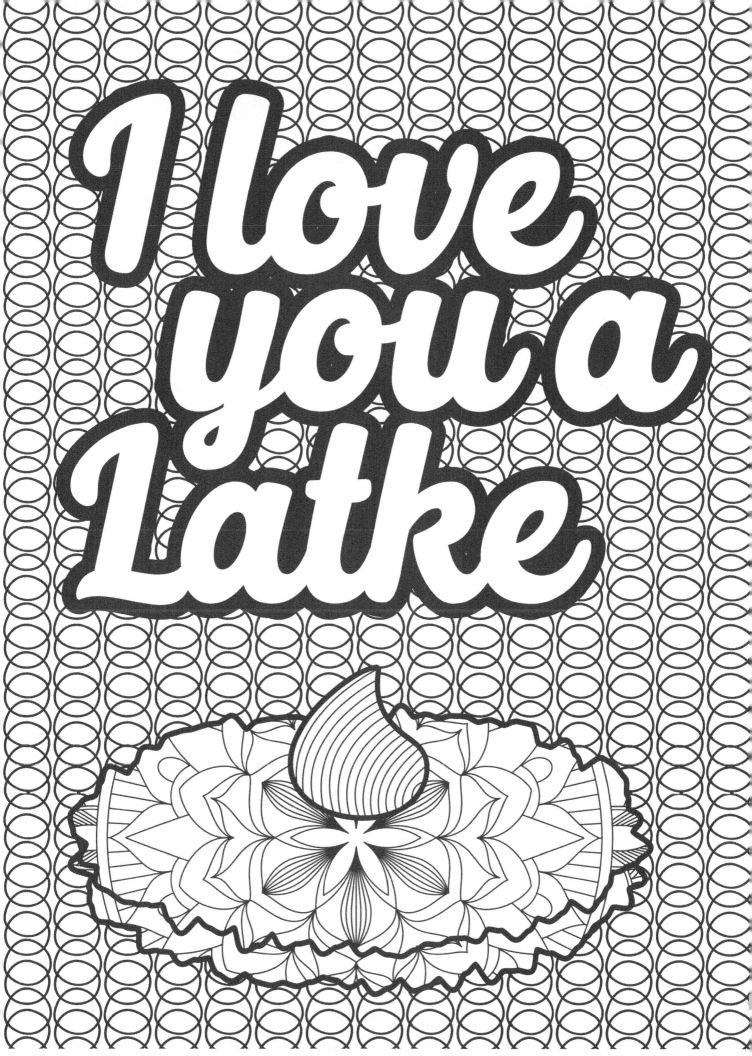

Made in the USA
Monee, IL
17 December 2019